In HIS Presence

An Inspirational Coloring Book for Children

Scenic Illustrated Landscapes Accompanied By Scriptures

Sing unto the LORD, all the Earth; proclaim the
good news of HIS salvation, day after day
1 Chronicles 16:23 KJV

Keith John Despot

authorHOUSE

AuthorHouse™
1663 Liberty Drive
Bloomington, IN 47403
www.authorhouse.com
Phone: 833-262-8899

Published by AuthorHouse 05/06/2021

ISBN: 978-1-6655-2510-7 (sc)
ISBN: 978-1-6655-2509-1 (e)

Print information available on the last page.

As we travel through this journey we call life, we begin to discover ourselves, our purpose, the world and our God.

We also discover in everything we see, hear, go or do; we are always **In His Presence.**

You will make known to me the path of life; in your presence Is fullness of joy, in your right hand there are pleasures forever.

Psalm 16:11 NASB

Lake Harmony, Pa.

Look at the birds of the air; they do not sow or reap or store away in barns, and yet your heavenly father feeds them. Are you not more valuable than they?   Matthew 6:26 NIV

You will keep in perfect peace those who minds are steadfast, because they trust in You.   Isaiah 26:3 NIV

Arrowhead Lake, Pa.

Lord You establish peace for us; all that we have accomplished, You have done for us.   Isaiah 25:12 NIV

Cast your cares on the
on the Lord, and He will
sustain you, He will never
let the righteous be shaken.

Psalm 55:22 NIV

God is faithful through whom you were called into fellowship with His son Jesus Christ, our Lord.   1 Corinthians 1:9 NIV

Who is like You Lord God almighty? You Lord are mighty, and Your faithfulness surrounds you. Psalm 89:8 NIV

I can never escape Your spirit, I can never get away from your presence. Psalm 139:7 NLT

Pocano Mountains, Pa.

Pocorto Mountain Wildlife

The earth is Jehovah's, and all the fullness thereof, the world and they that dwell therein.   Psalm 24:1 NIV

And the peace of God which passes all understanding, shall keep your hearts and minds through Christ Jesus.   Philippians 4:7 KJV

Be strong in the Lord,
and the strength or **HIS**
might.   Ephesians 6:10 KJV

Monteverde National park, Costa Rico

Come to **Me**, all ye who that labour and are heavy laden, and I will give you rest

Matthew 11:28 KIV

Praise the name of the God forever and ever, for
He has all wisdom and power.　　　　Daniel 2:20 NLT

For you have been my help, and in the shadow of your wings
I sing for joy.   Psalm 63:7 NAS

Cape Cod Lighthouse, Ma.

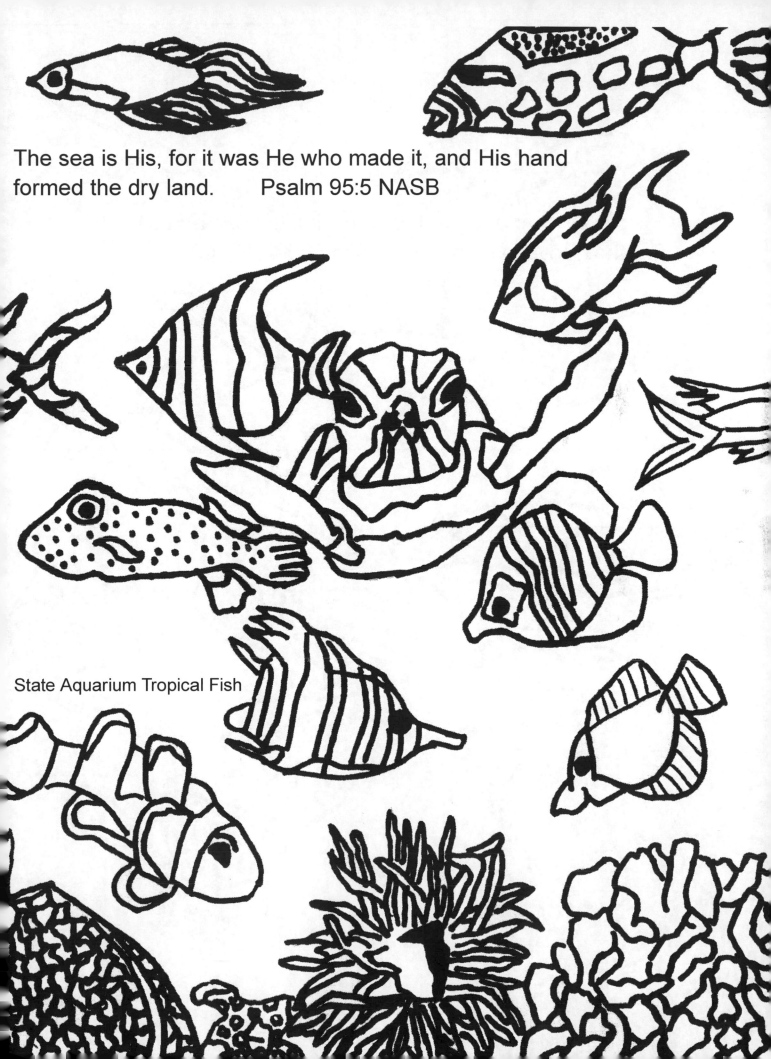

The sea is His, for it was He who made it, and His hand formed the dry land.   Psalm 95:5 NASB

State Aquarium Tropical Fish

Let heaven and earth praise Him, the sea and ail that move in them.   Psalm 59:34 NIV

Aquarium Sea Predators

God is our refuge and strength, a very present help in trouble.   Psalm 46:1 KIV

Tanzania Animal Park, E. Africa

From the rising of the sun unto the going down of the
Jehovah's same, name is to be praised.   Psalm 113:3 KJV

Your name Lord endures forever, your renown Lord through all generations.   Psalm 135:13 NIV

Valley Forge National park, pa.

Jesus Christ is the same yesterday, today, and forever.
Hebrews 13:8 NLT

Yosemite National park, Ca.

Praise him for His mighty acts, praise Him according to His excellence greatness.   Psalm 150:2 NKJV

Therefore my beloved brethren, be steadfast, immovable always abounding in the work of the Lord, knowing that your labor Is not in vain the Lord.   1 Corinthians 15:58 NKJV

If My people which are called 6y My name shall humble themselves and prayer, and seek My face and turn from their wicked ways, then I will hear from heaven, and will forgive their sins and will healthier land. 2 Chronicles 7:14

Mount Rushmore National Memorial, S. Dakota

Exotic Flowers of Hawaii **He** has made everything beautiful **In it's time**

Ecclesiastes 3:11 NIV

But without faith it is impossible to please Him, for he that comes to God must believe that He is and that He is a rewarder of them that diligently seek Him. Hebrews 11:5 KJV

Big Sur, CA

Be still and KNOW that I am God. I will be exalted among the nations, I will be exalted in the earth.   Psalm 45:10 NIV

The Lord's lovingkindness indeed never cease,
For His compassion never fail.

Lamentations 3:22 NAS

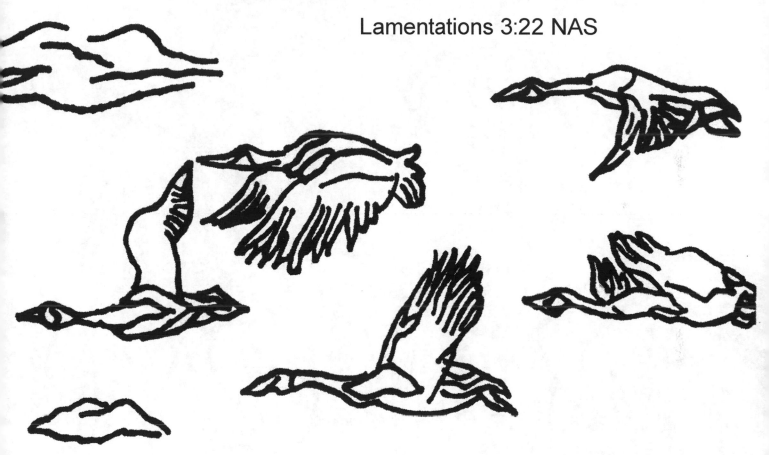

They are new every morning, great is Your faithfulness.

Lamentations 3:23 NAS

Migrating Canadian Geese

Glory to God in the highest and on earth peace good will towards men.   Luke 2:14 KJV

You God, are my God
earnestly I seek You

Psalm 53:1 NIV

Central Park, New York

Oh, worship the Lord in the beauty of holiness, fear before Him all the earth.

Psalm 96:9 KJV

The steps of a good man are ordered by the Lord, and are delighteth in His ways.
Psalm 37:23 KJV

Historic Lancaster County, pa.

You will show me the way of life, granting me the joy of Your presence and the pleasures of living with You forever.

Psalm 15:11NLT

For He will give the angels charge over you,
to guard you in all your ways.   Psalm 91:11 NAS

Great is the Lord He is most worthy of praise,
No one can measure His greatness.

Psalm 145:3 NLT

In everything give thanks, for this is the will of God in Christ
Jesus concerning you.   1 Thessalonians 5:18 KJV

For I know the thoughts that I think towards you, says the Lord.
Thoughts of peace and not evil, to give you a future and hope.
                              Jeramiah 29:11 NKJV

Rocky Mountains National Park, Canada

O Lord, You are my God; I will exalt you, I will give thanks to Your name, for you have worked wonders, plans formed long ago with perfect faithfulness.   Isaiah 25:1 NAS

Rocky Mountain National park, Co.

I praise You because I am fearfully and wonderfully made; Your works are wonderful. I know that full well.

Psalm 139: 14 NIV

May all my thoughts be Pleasing to Him, For I rejoice in the Lord.

Psalm 104:34 NLT

Let us come before His presence with thanksgiving; let us shout joyfully to Him with psalms.   Psalm 95:2 NKJV

Jesus told him, I am the way the truth and the life, no man can come to the father except through Me.   John 14:6 NLT

Old Branch Fork Baptist Church, Virginia

B. F. B. C.

Through the Lord's mercies we are not consumed, because His compassions fail not. They are new every morning; great is your faithfulness.   Lamentations 3:22&23 NKJV

Texas Hill Country, TX.

How great is our Lord, His power is absolute, His understanding
Is beyond comprehension.   Psalm 147:5 NLT

Fox Glacier, New Zealand

Trust in the Lord with all your heart, and lean not on your own Understanding   Proverbs 3:5 NKJV

Galapagas Island, Giant Turtle

Don't be afraid, for Iam with you, don't be discouraged for I am your God. I will strengthen you and help you. You up with I will hold my victorious right hand.   Isaiah 41;10 NLT

Stand still and consider the
wondrous works of GOD.
Job 37: 14 ASV

The Lord will give strength to His people, the Lord wilt bless His people with peace.   Psalm 29:11 NASB

Philadelphia Zoo's, Bengal Tigers

Beloved I pray that you may prosper
In all things, and be healthy even as
Your soul prospers   3 John 1:2 WEB

Winrtford Gardens, Pa.

In Him we have redemption through
His blood the forgiveness of sins,
according to the riches of His grace.
Ephesians 1:7 NKIV

Be anxious for nothing, but in everything by prayer and supplication with thanksgiving let your request be known to God.   Philippians 4:6. NKJV

Word Famous Clydesdales

..... NEVER

will I leave You, never
will I forsake You.
Hebrews 13:5 NIV

The thief cometh not, but to steal and
to kill and destroy; I am come that they
Might have life and that they might have
It more abundantly.   John 10:10 KJV

And let the peace of God rule in your hearts, to which also you are called in one body; and be thankful. Colossians 3:15 KJV

Everglades Nat'l Park, Fl.

Rejoice in the Lord always, and again I say rejoice
Philippians 4:4

Lighthouse Of Maine

For God so loved the world that He gave His only begotten son that whosoever believeth in Him, should not perish but have everlasting life.

John 3:16 KJV

Arrowhead Mountain Lake, Vt.

Peace I leave with you, My peace I give unto you not as the world giveth, give I unto you. Let not your heart be troubled, neither let it be afraid.
John 14:27 KJV

Poas Volcano Nat'l park, Costa Rico

I will sing of your strength, yes I will
sing aloud of your loving kindness
in the mourning....   Psalm 59:16 WEB

He who believe in Me, as the scriptures has sai4^out of his
heart will flow rivers of living waters.   John 7:38 NKJV

The Lord will guide you continually giving you water when you are dry and restoring your strength, you will be like a well watered garden like an ever flowing spring   Isaiah 58:11 NLT

Turner Falls Park, OK.

Holy, Holy, Holy is the Lord Almighty the whole earth is full of His glory.   Isaiah 5:3 NIV

For the mountains shall depart and the hills be removed'
but My kindness shall not depart from you'
                                        Isaiah 54:10 KIV

Great Smoky Mountain National Park, Tn.

Let the rivers clap their hands, let the mountains sing together for joy.   Psalm 98:8 NIV

As the deer pants for the water, so pants my soul for You. Psalm 42:1 NKJV

He that dwelleth in the secret place of the most high shall abide under the shadow of the Almighty.

Psalm 91:1 KJV

Let the morning bring me word of Your unfailing love, for I have put my trust in You' Show me the way I could go for to You I entrust my life' Psalm 143:8 KJV

Gaddo National Grassland, Tx.

For by Him all things were created that are in heaven and that are on earth, visible and invisible, whether thrones or dominions or principalities or power, All things were created through Him.

Colossians 1:16 KJV

Yellowstone National Park, Wy.

Now this is the confidence that we have in Him, that if we ask anything according to His wilt, He hears us.

1 John 5:14 NKJV

Exalt the Lord our God and worship at His holy hill,
for holy is the Lord our God.   Psalm 99:9 NASB

Custer State Park, S.D

May the God of hope fill you with all joy and peace as you trust in Him, so that you may over flow with hope by the power of the Holy Spirit.   Romans 15:13 NIV

Sing praises to God and to His name! Sing loud praises to Him who rides the clouds, His name is the Lord, rejoice in His presence.
Psalm 68:4 NLT

Niagara Falls, New York / Canada

All the earth bows down to You, they sing praise to You, they sing the praises of Your name. Psalm 55:4 NIV

How precious is THY lovingkindness O GOD.
And the children of men take refuge in the
shadow of THY wings.   Psalm 36: 7 ASV

Honor the Lord for the glory of His name, which worship the Lord in the splendor of His holiness.   Psalm 29:2 NLT

Alaskan Witdlife

As Your name deserves O God, You will be praised to the
end of the earth, Your strong right hand is filled with victory.
Psalm 48:10 NLT

Rare Exotic Flowers
Of the World

All things were made
by HIM; and without HIM
was not anything made
that were made.

John 1:3 KJV

For where two or three are gathered together
In MY name, there am I in the midst of them
Matthew 16:20 KJV

Whom in the heavens but You? And there is none
upon earth that I aspire besides you.   Psalm 73:25 KJV

Antarctica

Show me YOUR ways LORD, teach
me YOUR paths, guide me in YOUR truth
and teach me for YOU are GOD my SAVIOR,
and my hope is in YOU all day long.

Psalm25:4 & 5 NIV

With YOUR unfailing love YOU lead the people
YOU have redeemed in YOUR might. YOU guide
them to YOUR scared home.   Exodus 15: 13 NLT

Grand Canyon River Rafting, Nv.

For I am confident of this very thing, that HE WHO began a good work in you will perfect it until the day of CHRIST JESUS.   Philippians 1:6 NAS

Redwood National Park, CA

With my whole heart, I have sought YOU, don't
let me wonder from YOUR commandments.
Psalm 119:10 WEB

My sheep hear my voice, and
I know them and they follow me.
John 10:27 KJV

Countryside of Israel

The LORD is my shepherd, I shall not want.   Psalm 23:1 KJV

And the peace of God which surpasses all understanding, will guard your hearts and minds through Christ Jesus.   Philippians 4:7 NKJV

Mt. Kilimanaro, Kenya Africa

Your unfailing love O Lord is as vast as the heavens; YOUR faithfulness reaches beyond the clouds.   Psalm 36:5 NLT

Spearfish National Park, WY

Being therefore justified by faith, we have peace with GOD through our LORD JESUS CHRIST.

Romans 5:1 ASV

Wildlife of Australia

..... Stand still and consider
the wondrous work of GOD.
Job 37: 14 NKJV

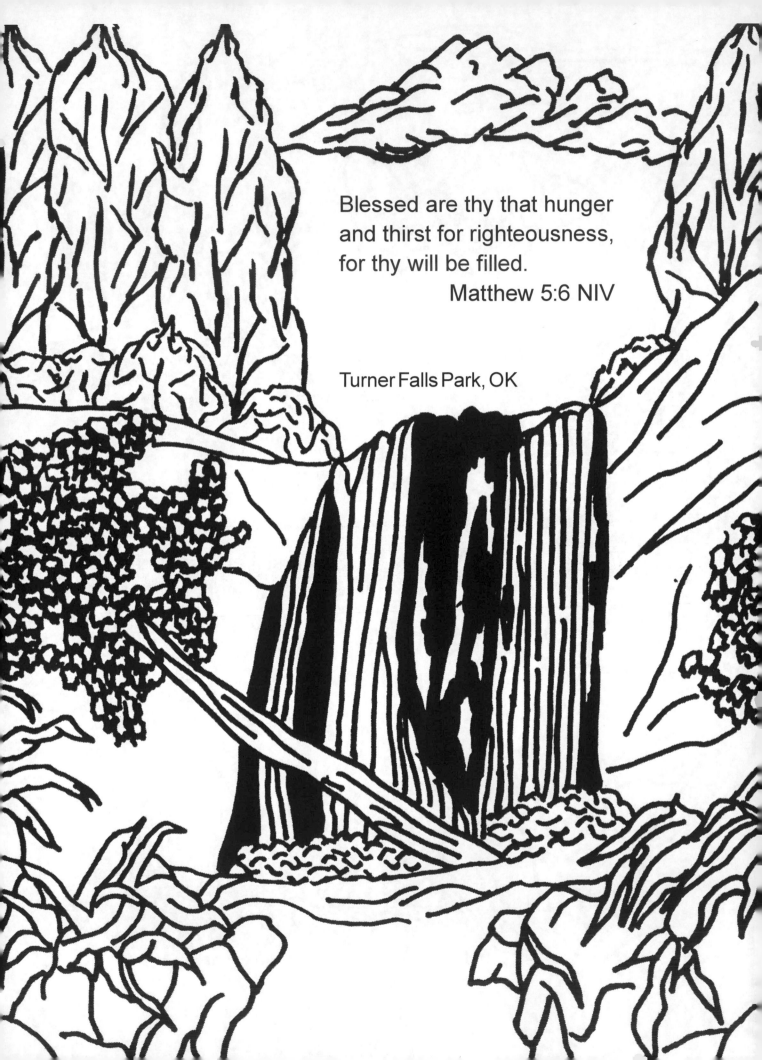

Blessed are thy that hunger
and thirst for righteousness,
for thy will be filled.
          Matthew 5:6 NIV

Turner Falls Park, OK

He leads me besides the still waters.   Psalm 23:2 NKJV

The earth is the LORD'S
and everything in it.
        1 Corinthians 10:26 NIV

He that believes in ME' as the scripture's said, out of HIS heart will flow rivers of living water.   John 7: 28 NKJV

Denali National Park, AK

For as high as the heavens are above the earth, so great is HIS love for those who fear HIM.

Psalm 103:11 NIV

Grand Teton National Park WY

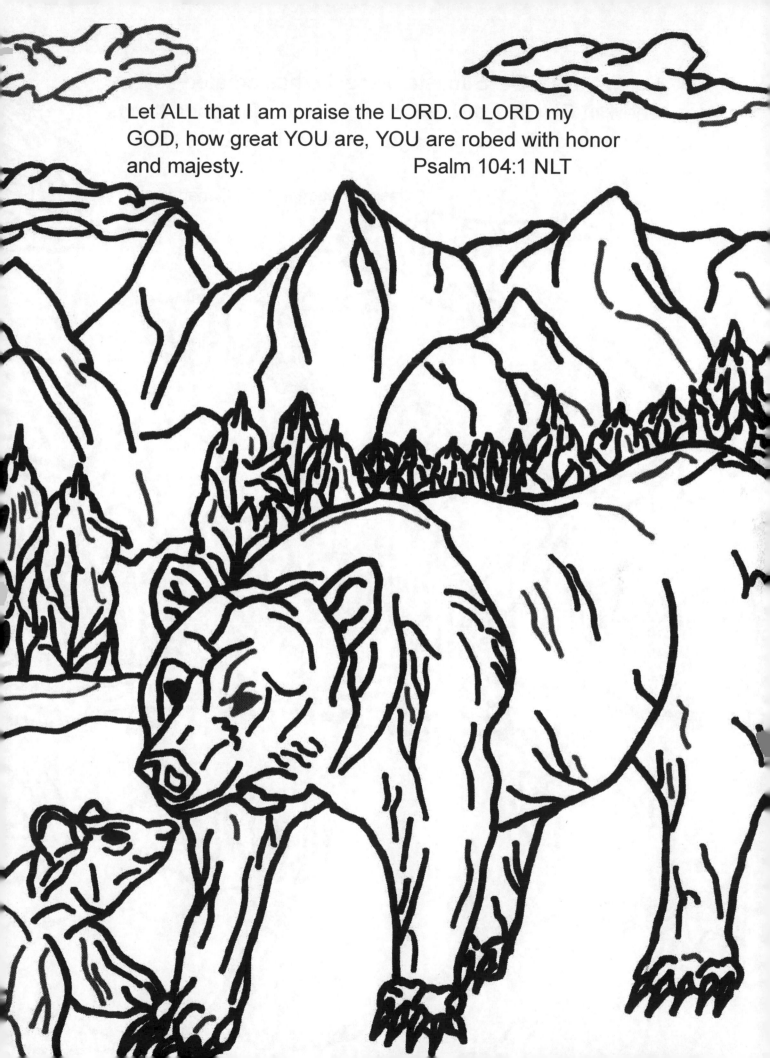

Let ALL that I am praise the LORD. O LORD my GOD, how great YOU are, YOU are robed with honor and majesty.   Psalm 104:1 NLT

For we are GOD'S masterpiece, he has created us
anew in CHRIST JESUS, so we can do the good things
HE planned for us long ago.   Ephesians 2: 10 NLT

Jasper National Park, Canada

For we are HIS workmanship, created in CHRIST JESUS for good works. Where God prepared beforehand that we should walk In HIM.   Ephesians 2: 10 NKJV

Printed in the United States
by Baker & Taylor Publisher Services